# *Keys to Successful Living*

## *A Contemporary Look at the Life and Ministry of Ezra, the Teacher Of the Law of God*

*By*
*Stan E. DeKoven*

Published by:

Vision Publishing

1115 D Street

Ramona, CA 92065

www.visionpublishingservices.com

1-800-9-VISION

All scripture references are taken from the NASB version of the Bible unless otherwise noted.
Printed in the United States of America

# TABLE OF CONTENTS

# Introduction

It is never too late to start building God's Vision for your life! Scripture tells us that Moses was at least 80 years of age when he *started* on his journey into the will of God for his life. If you have ever had the desire to serve God in your life, you must remember that He has never changed His mind about you!

We must remember, however, that God's dream and vision for our generation will be fulfilled as we work together, rather than as individuals, toward the goal. We must stay focused on reaching the nations of the world.

In Habakkuk 2:2 we read,

*"Record the **vision** and inscribe it on tablets, that the one who reads it may run"* (NASB).

We are required by God to share the vision or goals that He has laid out for us, with others in the Body of Christ.

Besides *vision*, the building of God's dream requires at least two additional things: trained and prepared *people* of vision, and the necessary *resources*.

Ezra, the scribe, was a man of great vision. He had a dream, a plan with its origins in the heart of God, for building the Kingdom of God for his day. As we look at Ezra we will discern vital patterns and principles that will assist us in building God's dream for us in our generation. Whether it be a church, a mission field, or a Bible College, the principles are the same as far as God is concerned.

# Chapter One

*A People Called of God*

*II Corinthians 3:6,*

*He has made us competent as **ministers of a new covenant,** not of the letter but of the Spirit; for the letter kills, but the Spirit gives life.*

*II Corinthians 3:17-18,*

*Now the Lord is the Spirit; and where the Spirit of the Lord is, there is freedom. And we, who with unveiled faces all reflect the Lord's glory, are being **transformed into his likeness** with ever-increasing glory, which comes from the Lord, who is the Spirit.*

*II Corinthians 4:1,*

*Therefore, since through God's mercy **we have this ministry,** we do not lose heart.*

We all want to fully accomplish what God intends for our lives. I have never met a person yet that selected failure as one of his or her primary goals in life. Everyone wants to succeed! All of God's people want to do well, to make a significant contribution to God's Kingdom. I find that people everywhere want success rather than mediocrity. They want to walk uprightly, excel at life, and enjoy happy relationships. They want to be a blessing to others.

Many people, however, do *not* feel like they are

succeeding. They are nobodies going nowhere, they think, having the deep notion that they have somehow been passed over in this life. Could it be that these people simply do not know *how* to achieve God's incredible goals for their lives?

God's Word gives many great examples of obedient servants, including men and women who were of simple or common heritage. Many may not have been particularly special. Some had no exceptional training, gifts or talents. They no doubt came in various sizes, shapes, and appearances: short, tall, overweight, slender, and perhaps even unattractive.

Elite birth is not a prerequisite for success. God frequently chooses the foolish things (or people) of this life to confound those who are considered high and wise. He chooses, anoints, and empowers people to achieve things greater than their biggest dreams. Against insurmountable odds, God frequently raises up the "common" folk to do a "not so common" work for His Kingdom.

## *An Example From the Word*

Just consider Simon Peter, a notorious man of great passion. He was not greatly educated, and often said the wrong thing at the right time. He, however, accomplished great things for God. He was incredibly enabled and empowered by the Holy Spirit to fulfill his calling in the Kingdom. (I continue to be amazed when people criticize Peter for failing to walk on the water. In fact, he *did* walk on the water, successfully at first. As believers, let us not be too quick to diagnose others' failures).

I think, further, about other incredible folks that God has used powerfully: Moses, Joshua, Daniel, Joseph, Esther or Deborah. Moses confronted Pharaoh when he was eighty years old! Joshua was well over eighty when he led Israel into the promised land. Our weaknesses and shortcomings do not seem to be a handicap to the God we serve.

## *Our Calling From God*

We need to fully realize that all of us have been called of God, according to the Word, as ministers in this New Covenant. We already have been called to the ministry of reconciliation, which is a fulltime effort. The real question we may ask ourselves is, what type of ministers are we going to be? This is not to question whether one should be a teacher, preacher or evangelist, for we have all been called to be witnesses or servants of the gospel wherever we are. We should be "able ministers" of the New Covenant. The question is, are we going to be able or not?

The era for saying, "I get Jesus through television or radio by myself," or "It's just Jesus and me," is gone. The time for mediocrity is past. The time for thinking that pew-sitters pass muster with God is history.

No "Lone Rangers" exist in the Body of Christ. You cannot separate the body from the head and maintain life. We need to be one with the Body of Christ, the Church, in order to flow and to function properly and powerfully.

We, godly men and women according to His Word, have been called to bring the message of salvation to the entire world. Yet ours is a difficult and troubled time in the history of the ages, not only in the US, but all around the planet. We believe, as has every generation, that we are in the last days. Many believe that we are going to see Jesus in our lifetime, though Scripture indicates that no one knows either the day or the hour, exactly. We do know, however, that we are closer today than we were yesterday.

There is a task that God has given directly to our generation. He has called us to reach a lost and dying world with the greatest message of all, the message of God's incredible love for all mankind. Thus, we must become fully prepared to fulfill our destiny, to fulfill God's vision and purpose for our lives.

# Chapter Two

## *Ezra's Historical Background*

In an effort to fully develop and exhibit the vision that God has for us, both individually and corporately, we must look to the Word of God for our examples. In Ezra's life and ministry we see much that is applicable to our generation's unique time and place in history. What is it about this mighty servant of the Lord that enabled him to play such a major role in the establishing of the people of God in his day and time?

## *A Captive People*

Ezra's time was historically a time of captivity for the people of God. They had been taken away from their blessed city of Jerusalem and the temple. They were held captive in Babylon for no less than 70 years.

In America we frequently say, "We live in a free country! This cannot really apply to us here!" We may be free, but only to a certain extent. In many insidious ways, we, like the children of Israel at Babylon, are captives. For example, the former Soviet Union requested of the Association of Christian Schools International, "Please, send us some trained Christian teachers to instruct us how to work with our public school children. We need you to teach us about Christian ethics and operation of our public school system. We need

Bibles and Christian teachers for our children in the local schools."

We do not have the freedoms that we think we have! They are becoming more and more limited! If you were to try to bring Bibles into one of *our* public schools in America, you might get thrown out on your ear! You have to admit that we, like the people in Ezra's time, are in a form of ungodly captivity. It is time that the Church wake up, recognize this, and begin the process of taking back that which the Devil has stolen!

Let us examine the details of Ezra's life, beginning in Ezra 7:1-10. We read,

> *Now after these things, in the reign of Artaxerxes, king of Persia, there went up Ezra son of Seraiah, son of Azariah, son of Hilkiah, son of Shallum, son of Zadok, son of Ahitub, son of Amariah, son of Azariah, son of Meraioth, son of Zerahiah, son of Uzzi, son of Bukki, son of Abishua, son of Phinehas, son of Eleazar, son of Aaron the chief priest. This Ezra went up from Babylon, and he was a scribe skilled in the law of Moses, which the LORD God of Israel had given; and the king granted him all he requested because the hand of the LORD his God was upon him. And some of the sons of Israel and some of the priests, the Levites, the singers, the gatekeepers, and the temple servants went up to Jerusalem in the seventh year of King Artaxerxes. And he came to Jerusalem in the fifth month, which was in*

*the seventh year of the king. For on the first of the first month he began to go up from Babylon; and on the first of the fifth month he came to Jerusalem, because the good hand of his God was upon him. For Ezra had set his heart to study the law of the LORD, and to practice it, and to teach His statutes and ordinances in Israel (NASB).*

As a young man, Ezra was a man of significant might and courage. A contemporary of Nehemiah who rebuilt the walls of Jerusalem, Ezra understood his time and place. He was one of many in his day with the potential for greatness. Like Caleb of old, he was a man of a *"different spirit."* Even so, Ezra, a captive, had no guarantee that he would ever be able to fulfill his desire to minister the Word of God and to see Jerusalem rebuilt. In spite of the reality of his situation, Ezra began to prepare for what he believed God planned to do. Likewise, before we see a great outpouring of God's Spirit, there will first come a time of initial preparation.

## Gifting of God and Investment

God is no fool when it comes to stewardship. He invests wisely into His Body. If God gives you a gift, it is because He knew He could trust you with the investment of that treasure in your life. The Apostle Paul said, *"We have this treasure in earthen vessels, that the excellency of the power may be of God and not of us" (2 Corinthians 4:7 KJV).* This treasure is very precious and costly. It includes not only the eternal life of God, but also any of the gifts or abilities He gives to us as individuals. They are not for us to hoard personally, but to use for the building of the Body of Christ and for reaching our lost and dying world. Thus, you and I will be held accountable for the development and proper use of every gift that God has deposited within our lives.

Ezra had no real indication that he would ever be able to fulfill his destiny. But, he still trained and prepared himself. He was a scribe and priest, and an overseer or judge. He had many talents and capabilities. He trained in the things of God with others of the Captivity in Babylon with him.

Yet, Ezra was little different than any of the other little Jewish boys in his generation. He happened to be of the Aaronic lineage of Priesthood. What separated him from the rest, however, was the determination of his own heart. He determined that he was not going to be mediocre! He was not going to be second class! He understood that, though he had nothing special within himself, His God was "special" enough. If his God were with him, all things would be possible!

### Gaining Skills

Ezra 7:6 tells us specifically of Ezra: *"He was a scribe **skilled** in the law of Moses."*

Why did he learn his skills? Because of the determination that he made in his heart. He understood that *"the hand of the LORD his God was upon him" (verse 6).*

## Being Dealt the Good Hand of the Lord

If you will do anything for God, make sure that His hand is upon you! You need to know this! Many times Christians will spend their efforts attempting to do something for God. Their desires are to do well, but their approach to God's work is misguided. They will start something and then ask God to bless it. They do not even take the time to ask, "By the way, Lord, is this something *You* want me to do?" It is a formula for disaster.

Ezra was not that way. He understood his need to hear the voice of God. He understood that he needed to prepare himself. We need the hand of God in our lives now more than ever. We need to know that the Spirit of God is speaking to us in the Church. We need to know that God is indeed with us in our endeavors. But in order to know that, we need to stop and *ask* Him first. It is so much better to get the mind of Christ and hear the voice of the Holy Spirit *before* we move ahead with our efforts.

# Chapter Three

*Get Ready, Get Set*

*"Ezra had set his heart to study the Law of the Lord, and to practice it and to teach His statutes and ordinances in Israel" (Ezra 7:10).*

This verse contains the keys to Ezra's success, and to ours. As a young man, in spite of his circumstances or the culture of his day, Ezra *set* his heart to study the Law of the Lord.

The Hebrew word for *set* is the word *"Koom"*. It means: to be prepared, to be faithful, firm, and established, to make ready spiritually. It tells us how he *set* his heart.

## *The Setting and the Plate*

I was a baseball catcher for many years. I have always had the build for it, somewhat like a fire hydrant.

I felt that when I was catcher, home plate "belonged" to me. It was, in my estimation, mine and mine alone. I took it very personally if someone on the wrong team attempted to come across *"my plate!"*

Because of my feeling of ownership, I devised all kinds of ingenious ways to keep people off *"my plate!"* I would disguise it by kicking dirt on it, in hopes that they would miss it as they attempted to come home. If someone tried to slide in, I put my body in the way. I have monstrous thighs and I could set myself like a rock. I *dared* the poor individual to cross *"my plate."* Sometimes, I got belted. I belted back a few times too, which was a whole lot more fun, for me at least! I so determined in myself to stop the runner that I saw myself as immovable.

This highly developed sense of ownership of home plate was *"set"* in my thinking! When a player attempted to cross *"my plate"* from third base, something would begin to rise up within me to deny him that privilege.

This is the force of the word in this passage, *"Ezra set himself."* He set his mind, his eye, and his entire self on the goal, and he did not waver.

But Ezra also did more than that.

## *The Heart of the Matter*

Scripture reveals that *"Ezra set his **heart.**"* He set the very center of who he was on doing some specific things for the Kingdom of God. There are many things on which we can set our hearts. For instance, we can set our hearts, as politicians do, on winning a political office. Perhaps it is the power of the office which is the heart's goal, or perhaps fame, money, success, relationships, or educational degrees. "If only I had a degree," one might moan. "Then I would escape my poverty!"

We see here that Ezra set his **heart** on that which was best, the study of the Law. The first thing we also need to know is what God is saying about our lives. Then we need to allow His Word to do its work in and through us!

## Getting the Word of the Lord

You cannot gain the Word of the Lord by osmosis. You cannot sit with the Bible open on top of your head and think that, somehow, the Word of the Lord will soak through. You cannot get the Word of the Lord by simply sitting in a congregation somewhere and hearing the Word preached! The anointing upon the spoken Word is not enough! You must, must, must, study the Word of God, personally, to receive the word of the Lord for yourself. We see this principle in II Timothy 2:15:

*"Study to show thyself approved unto God, a workman that needeth not to be ashamed, rightly dividing the Word of Truth" (KJV).*

Ezra set his focus upon the Word of God. He may have prayed to the Lord, "The one thing that I want more than anything else is: *GOD, I WANT TO KNOW YOUR WORD!"*

One key to success is always the knowledge of the Word! We *must* store God's Word in our hearts; the Word will change and transform our lives for the Kingdom of God's sake! The mind that is illumined by the Word is able to receive the revelation of the Lord as it flows from Him towards us. We need more revelation from the Lord in these days of trouble than ever before.

## Practice Makes Perfect

From our passage we also see that Ezra did not just set his heart to learn the Word of the Lord, but he also did something with his knowledge. He decided to practice it!

*"For Ezra had set his heart to study the Law of the Lord, and to **practice** it and to teach His statutes and ordinances in Israel"* *(Ezra 7:10).*

Note two aspects of Ezra's practicing that are worth considering: first, he wanted to live according to God's Word, to do justly, love mercy, and walk with humility. And beyond that, he was in pursuit of excellence as a scribe and priest.

Scribes, because of their trade, always worked with meticulous accuracy, as close to perfection as was humanly possible. Ezra learned to pay close attention to detail and was fully disciplined in his study. This was no place for "sloppy agape." He studied and did all as best he could. He not only applied himself to know the Word, but also to live according to God's plan.

More than simply practicing obedience, he was practicing the very activities that he would be performing if ever he was released into the ministry that God called him to do.

## Start Small, Wherever You Are

At twelve years of age I was a new believer. It was not long until I received the call of God to full-time ministry. At that time God also indicated that it would not be a "typical ministry." I knew immediately that my calling from God meant that I needed to prepare myself. I needed to set my heart to prepare for ministry.

Since my ministry was to include the preaching and teaching of the Word, I practiced preaching wherever and to whomever I could. I even practiced on my family dog! In my mind, every time I preached to that dog, he got saved. I learned how to preach and bring deliverance by "delivering" my dog! In fact, God actually healed my dog of a goiter! It was the first miracle God did in terms of my personal ministry. I commanded the goiter to go away in the *Name of Jesus*, and it did! I am so glad that God graciously responded to a little child's faith.

Are you called to preach? Start by practice-preaching to the windshield as you drive to work! Many of my best sermons have first been preached to my windshield!

We *must* practice! I require all aspiring ministers to teach Sunday school. They all want to preach. They may say to me, "I want to get out there and preach the Word, Brother!" But if you cannot communicate well with children you may never do well with adults! Jesus certainly included ministry to children as an important facet of His work here on earth.

Ezra sought the opportunities to practice his ministry. You also do well to seek out the opportunities to practice your ministry in different places. If someone telephones saying, "I'm sick," you have an open door to go and lay hands on him and heal him in Jesus' Name! Has not God given us that power and authority?

Jesus promised that if we were faithful in little things He would **make** us rulers over much! At some point you and I must get out of our boats and begin to take steps in ministry for the Lord. That means action, practice, practice and practice! After faithfulness in these little things, God will use you in the big things He plans to do in and through you, which are more than you could ever imagine!

### *Little Becomes Much*

Jesus said, *"If you are faithful in little things, I will make you rulers over much."* Ezra also practiced his priestly duties. He practiced preaching the Word and teaching. He practiced ordaining people. He practiced laying hands on people. He practiced anointing them with oil. I would not be surprised if he just grabbed anybody available and said, "You just stand there and let me pray for you." Because he had set his heart, he knew that the day would come when God would call upon him to serve. He wanted to be ready for that time.

### *Cleanliness Counts*

Part of the concept of practice is dealing with issues of our own hearts.

*Wherefore lay apart all filthiness and superfluity of naughtiness, and receive with meekness the engrafted word, which is able to save your souls. But be ye doers of the word, and not hearers only, deceiving your own selves" James 1:21-22 (NASB).*

God is speaking to the Church in our day: *"Prepare your hearts. Not just your minds, businesses, and families, but prepare your hearts as well, for I am ready to move."* This is really the prophetic word to the Church of our day.

God is saying to the Church, "Prepare!" because He is beginning to pour out His Spirit. When He pours His Spirit out in full, He wants to use the Body that presently exists. That is you and me. He will not raise up some other body for His purpose, but will use us to minister His Word in power. I believe we will see His signs and wonders, but we need to prepare and clean up within our hearts!

I do not want to miss the next wave of His outpouring. We have been in somewhat of a holding phase in the church; I doubt that holding time will "hold" much longer! I believe when God begins to move He will move quickly. He will move through those individuals who have prepared to receive from Him, and have applied themselves diligently in preparation for their work assignment from God.

*These Things Do and Teach*

Thirdly, Ezra set his heart upon teaching the Word of God. He did not stop at learning knowledge and practicing it. He actively sought the opportunities where he could teach, proclaim, and transfer that knowledge gained from studious application of the Word of God.

When I get a revelation from God's Holy Scripture, I want to share it with someone. Why? Because it was not given to me just to hoard for myself. On rare occasions those who move in prophetic ministry might receive a prophecy from God with the proviso, "You need to hold this until a more appropriate time." Usually, however, when God gives a revelation from His Word, it is so that you may share it immediately with others.

We usually go to church prepared to receive something from the minister for our hearts. We believe that he has been studying the Word diligently the previous week, and expect that he in fact *does* have something fresh from God. If we did not believe that, we would not attend in the first place.

If you heard that the preacher had merely called a sermon service and asked them to ship him three or four different sets of sermon notes, would you care to listen so intently? And if he glanced over one of the four sermons and said, "Oh, I think this one looks good enough for them," and preached it, there would be no anointing, no unction of the Holy Ghost, no signs, wonders, or miracles. If you never returned, that would be quite understandable. If there is no anointing, why go? Why be a part of something void of God's presence?

We all attend church with an expectation that we will receive something from God. When you receive from God, He wants you to take it and pass it on to someone else. He wants you to give it to somebody, with the joy of the Lord flowing from your heart. Spiritually speaking, Ezra was responding to the same godly prompting.

The Hebrew word for *teach* means to train, to drive like one drives an ox, or to set the limits or boundaries within which people travel. The teaching of the Word, when done under the anointing of God, pushes, guides, and directs us, narrowing our focus so that we will know clearly the direction in which God wants us to walk.

That is exactly what Ezra wanted to do. He understood that the people were in captivity, in bondage. They somehow believed that their poverty and oppression were what they deserved.

Guaranteed, the Babylonians were just like the Egyptians that had held Israel captive years before. I am sure that they wanted God's people to believe that what they were experiencing was the very best that they could ever expect out of this life.

How often have we in the Church heard the same message? How often have we heard the message about being born in the wrong neighborhood, the wrong place, the wrong time, or the wrong circumstances? We are told in no uncertain terms, "God cannot use you."

Let us understand our gracious Lord: God can use anybody He wants to! *He* is the boss, not circumstances.

How happy to realize that God looked down through the annals of time and chose *you* to be alive in this exact place and time, because He wanted you here. He knew, "I cannot find anyone better." You are His best pick for the job in your area at this time, simply because He put you here. God has placed His Spirit on the inside of you for this very purpose.

Ezra knew that all the people around him were being indoctrinated into the belief system that said, "We are stuck here in Babylon, we might as well just make the best of it. We are never going to leave here!" God, however, had a greater plan. God *always* has a greater plan.

I can look at the geopolitical situation in our world and honestly tell you, "Jesus Christ is still Lord." I can see the breakdown of the family in my own nation, the breakdown of the infrastructure of its cities and all the discouraging news, and yet I can confidently proclaim, "Jesus is still Lord." I can further tell you, without reservation, that Jesus Christ is going to establish His Kingdom, using us to do it.

We are "world changers," because that same Spirit that raised Christ from the dead dwells in us. Let us be like Ezra! He set his heart despite dire circumstances, and avoided the mentality that he was a perpetual captive in Babylon. We are "world changers," not just waiting for our exit visas to come through so that we can be translated out of this miserable existence to heaven. Praise God, some day there will come the time when we leave and go to heaven. In the meantime, there is a lot of work that needs to be done in the Kingdom of God!

Ezra could have kicked back and waited, sitting around hoping for change. Rather, Ezra got up and began to do something about his circumstances. He set himself to study, to do, and to teach.

What are you going to do? You can sit around, or, like Ezra, you can begin to prepare yourself. You can begin to narrow your own boundaries, trim some of the superfluity out of your life, and begin dealing with the issues of purity in your heart.

Allow the Word to begin speaking to you now. You can allow yourself to be trained and prepared; why not do it now? You can become more than you ever thought you could be; why not start now? Is not God able? Why not become all that God created you to be?

## More Than Able

God can and will meet us where we are and empower us for greatness, if only we set our hearts on Him, first *to study* His Word, then *to practice* it, and finally *to teach* it, to narrow and set limits upon ourselves.

We need the grounding obtained through the Word of God. We need the grounding gotten through practice. We need the grounding attained as we teach and minister the Word.

History reveals that Ezra did not prepare himself in vain. God never lays a burden on one's heart just for the sake of giving a useless burden. Have you ever wondered to yourself, "Why do we talk about building a multi-million dollar world ministry center on this Earth? Why, if Jesus may come back tomorrow? Why waste the money when we could just hang onto it 'til Jesus comes?"

God gives visions to people because He intends to fulfill them! Does that mean Jesus cannot come back within the next ten years if a particular God-given project would take ten years to complete? Suppose Jesus comes back for His Church within five years and the ten-year project is yet incomplete, did we waste our time, effort, and resources? Absolutely not! There will be plenty of time to finish that goal or vision and put it to full, beneficial use when Jesus Christ establishes His throne here on Earth. The Church will need many ministry headquarters throughout this planet to do the work of God in the future. It will be the most exciting, successful, and expansive time the Family of Almighty God has ever known. God has big plans for you and me. God is no fool, He is investing in you!

During our time you and I must also be investing wisely in the Kingdom of God. We must invest ourselves to see God's work go forward in our generation. Ezra did. He was so determined within his own heart that he was unimpressed by the apparently impossible circumstances surrounding him.

# Chapter Four

## *The Incredible Results*

Shortly after Ezra set his heart and prepared himself, God began to open the doors for him. God favored him because His *"good hand"* was upon him. In Nehemiah 8:1-6, we see a picture of what God can do, even with simple folk who will commit themselves to the path of success; that is, to a greater cause than the pursuit of their own happiness.

*And all the people gathered as one man at the square which was in front of the Water Gate, and they asked Ezra the scribe to bring the Book of the Law of Moses which the LORD had given to Israel. Then Ezra the priest brought the law before the assembly of men, women, and all who could listen with understanding, on the first day of the seventh month. And he read from it before the square which was in front of the Water Gate from early morning until midday, in the presence of men and women, those who could understand; and all the people were attentive to the Book of the Law. And Ezra the scribe stood at a wooden podium which they had made for the purpose. And beside him stood Mattithiah, Shema, Anaiah, Uriah, Hilkiah, and Maaseiah on his right hand; and Pedaiah, Mishael, Malchijah, Hashum,Hashbaddanah, Zechariah, and*

*Meshullam on his left hand. And Ezra opened the book in the sight of all the people, for he was standing above all the people; and when he opened it, all the people stood up. Then Ezra blessed the LORD, the great God. And all the people answered, "Amen, Amen!" while lifting up their hands; then they bowed low and worshipped the LORD with their faces to the ground (Nehemiah 8:1-6 NASB).*

From the context given earlier in Nehemiah 7:39-42 (which gives a numerical register of the incredible company of people returning from captivity), it is interesting to note that a huge number of priests with their families were attending this meeting. The families of the Levitical priesthood alone numbered in the thousands.

The context clearly shows that others in leadership at that time recognized the true anointing of God on a life that was prepared by God. So it was so and should it be today. Note the fourth verse:

*And Ezra the scribe stood at a wooden podium which they had made for the purpose. And beside him stood Mattithiah, Shema, Anaiah, Uriah, Hilkiah, and Maaseiah on his right hand; and Pedaiah, Mishael, Malchijah, Hashum, Hashbaddanah, Zechariah, and Meshullam on his left hand.*

Only one priest out of many was singled out for

the task of reading the Word of God to the people. Perhaps many of the priests felt qualified but only one, Ezra, was fully prepared for the revival that was to come.

The Bible states that from early morning until late in the day, Ezra stood behind a specially made pulpit, reading and clearly explaining God's Word. So commanding was the anointing upon the Word and Ezra that every ear was tuned to him.

*Then Ezra blessed the LORD the great God. And all the people answered, "Amen, Amen!" while lifting up their hands; then they bowed low and worshipped the LORD with their faces to the ground (NASB).*

We can almost see the entire congregation of thousands, standing in awe-filled reverence as Ezra opened the Book of the Law to read. As he spoke the blessing, the people fell on their faces and worshipped God.

Ezra led in praise and worship to the Lord and God's people responded as he ministered the Word. Ezra carefully expounded God's precious "Manna from heaven" to open, hungry hearts. The people stood and remained standing all the while, as Ezra taught the meaning and sense of the Law of God in clear, concise, understandable words.

Finally, under the anointed teaching of Ezra, the conviction of the Holy Spirit fell. The people wept, which is often the case when we know that we have displeased God. Yet, the anointing was so great that at the command of Ezra, the weeping ceased and shouts of joy rang forth. "Truly, the joy of the Lord is our strength!" became their cry.

## A Final Thought

The ministry of this particular service continued for eight days (verse 18). This happened on a national scale and every person capable of understanding spoken language attended.This incident was the beginning of a great revival in Israel. It was accompanied by formal repentance and celebration that crossed every strata of society. Marriages were restored. Families were healed. Wrongs were set right. People began sending gifts to each other in appreciation of God's demonstrated intent to bring complete and total restoration to His people.

Ezra became a powerful leader, used by God to bring national revival to Israel. He played his proper role and vitally affected the plan and purpose of God for his generation. God recorded it for us in these two Old Testament books as an example for our admonition:

*"Now these things happened to them as an example, and they were written for our instruction, upon whom the ends of the ages have come" (1 Corinthians 10:11 NASB).*

God is looking for Ezras today, men and women who will set their hearts to know the Lord, know His Word, and to be transformed through that Word. Those who thoroughly practice God's principles, are enabled to teach His Word with awesome power, bringing heavenly results. May God help us all to learn and apply these Keys to Success -- until Jesus comes!

# Chapter Five

## *Conclusions to Be Drawn*

We, the Church, must become a people of commitment. We must *set* our *hearts* to *learn*, to *do*, and to *teach* the Word of the Lord.

We must stand up against the opposition of the enemy, the opposition of others, and the opposition of our own weakness and fear to *set our hearts intently upon learning, doing, and teaching* the Word of the Lord.

*Ezra had set his heart to study the law of the LORD, and to practice it, and to teach His statutes and ordinances in Israel (Ezra 7:10).*

*Ezra opened the book in the sight of all the people for he was standing above all the people; and when he opened it, all the people stood up (Nehemiah 8:5).*

*Then Ezra blessed the LORD the great God. And all the people answered, "Amen, Amen!" while lifting up their hands; then they bowed low and worshipped the LORD with their faces to the ground (Nehemiah 8: 6).*

It is time for the Ezras of our generation to seriously seek the Lord. We must all prepare to take our places as able ministers of the New Covenant. Prepare now. Now is the time to study and learn, to practice and do what we learn, and teach and preach the good news at every opportunity. Preparation and obedience will open the doors for revival on a national and even planetary scale. God is waiting for us to do our part. Are you preparing? Are you ready?

# Keys to Success Outline for Review:

I. Introduction:

  A. All want to fulfill their destiny in God.

  B. God's Word is filled with people who completed great things for the Kingdom of God.

   1. They overcame insurmountable odds.

   2. They were humble.

   3. They were obedient.

   4. They were men and women of the Word.

  C. Great Biblical examples, both men and women:

   Jesus, Joshua, Esther, Deborah, Daniel, Joseph, the Apostles, Stephen, and martyrs of the faith (Heb. 11).

II. We are all called to be people of the Word, doing great things for the Kingdom of God.

  A. Ezra was such a man, an example for us today.

  B. He achieved great things for the Kingdom against insurmountable odds in his day and age.

III. Ezra's Historical Background: (Ezra 7:1-10)

  A. A contemporary of Nehemiah

  B. A scribe and a priest

  C. A captive in Babylon

  D. Trained in the things of God with others

E. Distinguished himself through faithfulness "Study to shew thyself approved..." (2 Tim 2:15).

IV. Just as Ezra and Esther were brought to the forefront of the Kingdom "for such a time as this," so are we in the Church today.

A. "God's good hand was upon him."

B. "He *SET* his heart," *kuwm: reposed, faithful, firm, established, to make ready spiritually.*

C. "He set his *HEART:*" focused his attention and centered himself on the Word of God.

1. *Studied* it (2 Tim. 2:15).

2. *Practiced* it (James 2:21-22).

a) Put away the things of the flesh.

b) A doer of the Word, not just a hearer.

3. *Taught* it. He set boundaries.

V. The Results (Nehemiah 8:1-8)

A. Ezra read and taught the Word of God clearly to the people at the founding of the temple.

B. He stood in the authority and the anointing for which God had prepared him.

C. The fear and reverence of the Lord was manifest in the House of God in that day.

D. The Awe and Worship of God came over the people. The presence of God was manifested. National repentance and revival resulted.

VI. Conclusions:

A. We must all become a people with our hearts set on preparing for the call of God upon our lives.

1. *Set* our *hearts* on the Word of God.

2. *Study* and *learn* the Word of God.

3. *Practice* what we learn.

4. *Teach* what we have learned and practiced.

# About Vision International Ministries

At Vision International University, we are involved with the work of God around the world. The college opened in 1974 on the tiny island of Tasmania, off the south of Australia. Dr. Ken Chant began a ministry training program because of a great revival burning in Australia. Many churches were coming into being without the benefit of pastors or leadership to shepherd the people of God. A correspondence training program was started for the development of literally thousands of Christian leaders, whose primary function became the shepherding of the flock of God.

Simultaneously in the states, Dr. Joseph Bohac and I (18 years old at the time) began a training program at our church. It was called the *Logos Bible Institute*. It was much like the Bible College campuses that we have established around the world today. It was a group of local church people who were being trained on how to minister the power of God effectively and dynamically to the community surrounding them. Counselor training was a primary function along with Bible College training.

In 1990, we became a full university program with five different colleges, each being a portion of the overall ministry of Vision International University/Vision International University.

Our primary assignment and function as given

by God is to plant Bible Colleges within the local Church. Why? Because it is the Church which is the model of New Testament ministry that Jesus came to birth, the place where ministry preparation is to occur.

It is apparent in Christ's training of the disciples that God's intent is to move through the local Church. We do not have the benefits of Jesus' physical presence with us as pastor and teacher, but we do have His gifts and His anointing. We find these in the local Church. That is where the anointing is at its greatest.

God has helped us establish over 100 Bible College campuses in the US and in nearly 50 different nations. We raise up Christian leadership in the local Church.

One example of the need for training is Europe. Great revival is occurring in Europe, but local churches are not prepared to assimilate additional people. Reports from Romania state that up to five new churches per week are opening. Between the Pentecostal and Baptist denominations, there are over 4000 churches in Romania, but only 400 trained pastors.

We use the term *"trained"* very loosely. In Europe, leadership positions are being assigned based on the length of time since the individual's initial salvation experience. It is not unusual for people to go to one and say, "You've been saved for six months! Be our pastor! Come teach us everything you know!" Unqualified people have a hard time in the leadership positions that God has ordained to be operative in the local church. There is indeed a desperate need worldwide to raise up leadership.

Even here in the U.S., there is a tremendous need to raise up leaders within the local Church and send them out in Five-fold ministry teams, as ordained by God through the examples of His churches at Antioch and Ephesus.

Training in the early Church was accomplished through the auspices of the local Church. It was done under the authority of the Apostles, Prophets, Pastors, Evangelists, and Teachers. After the training was completed, the Holy Spirit spoke and said, *"Set apart for Me "_____" for the work to which I have called them."*

We are successfully doing this through Church-based Bible Colleges. God is raising up new churches through His own plan for expanding the Kingdom!

This is the *VISION* of Vision International Ministries. We provide the proven structures for training the people of God to move forward and be productive in their ministries and communities. For those having no program within their local church, we offer the opportunity of full and effective training through our external student program. For those churches which do not have a training plan yet established within their community, we have many exciting ways of getting you started. Our experience has been that when the people of God grow in their training and spiritual walk, there is a corresponding growth in the local church.

*Are you prepared? Are your people prepared? What are you doing about it?*

1. Set your heart.
2. Study and learn.
3. Practice what you learn.
4. Teach what you learn.
5. God's will shall be done in the earth as you practice the *Keys to Success*.

May we help you to start in the right direction?

*For further information regarding training and educational programs, along with their potential, please fill out and mail the attached response card.*

Name:_____

Address:_____

City:_____

State:_____

Zip:_____ Phone:_____

I am interested in:

_ Completing my Christian Education

_ Books from Vision Christian Ministries

_ Tapes on this or any other subject of importance

_ Learning about Christian Counseling

_ other items or issues_____

# The Teaching Ministry of Dr. Stan E. DeKoven

Dr. Stan DeKoven conducts seminars and professional workshops, both nationally and internationally, based on his books and extensive experience in Practical Christian Living. He is available for limited engagements at church seminars, retreats and conferences. For more information and a complete topical listing of books, we invite you to contact him:

**Dr. Stan DeKoven, President**
**Vision International University**
**Walk in Wisdom Seminars**
**1115 D Street**
**Ramona, CA 92065**
**760-789-4700 (in California) or**
**1-800-9 VISION**

# Other helpful books by Dr. DeKoven

- *40 Days to the Promise: A Way Through the Wilderness*
- *Addiction Counseling*
- *Assessment in Counseling*
- *Catch The Vision*
- *Christian Education*
- *Crisis Counseling*
- *Family Violence: Patterns of Dysfunction*
- *From a Father's Heart*
- *Grief Relief*
- *Healing Community*
- *Homiletics*
- *I Want to be Like You Dad*
- *Journey Through the New Testament*
- *Journey Through the Old Testament*
- *Journey to Wholeness: Restoration of the Soul*
- *Marriage and Family Life: A Christian Perspective*
- *New Beginnings*
- *On Belay! Introduction to Christian Counseling*
- *Parenting On Purpose*
- *Pastoral Ministry*
- *Prelude to a Requiem*
- *Setting the House in Order*
- *Supernatural Architecture*

- *That's the Kingdom of God*
- *Transferring the Vision*
- *Twelve  Steps to Wholeness*
- *Visionary Leadership*

www.ingramcontent.com/pod-product-compliance
Lightning Source LLC
Chambersburg PA
CBHW060202070426
42447CB00033B/2310